Colors

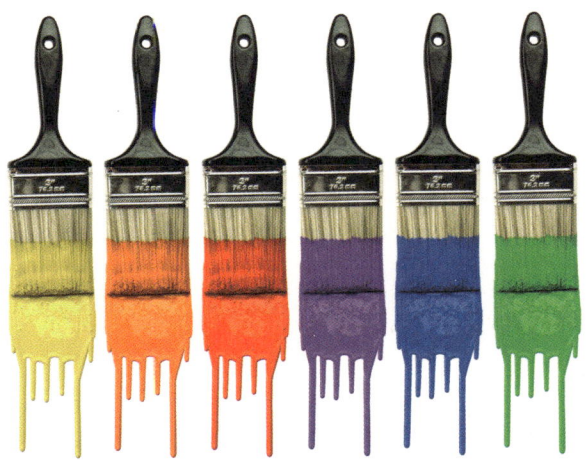

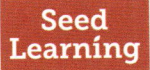

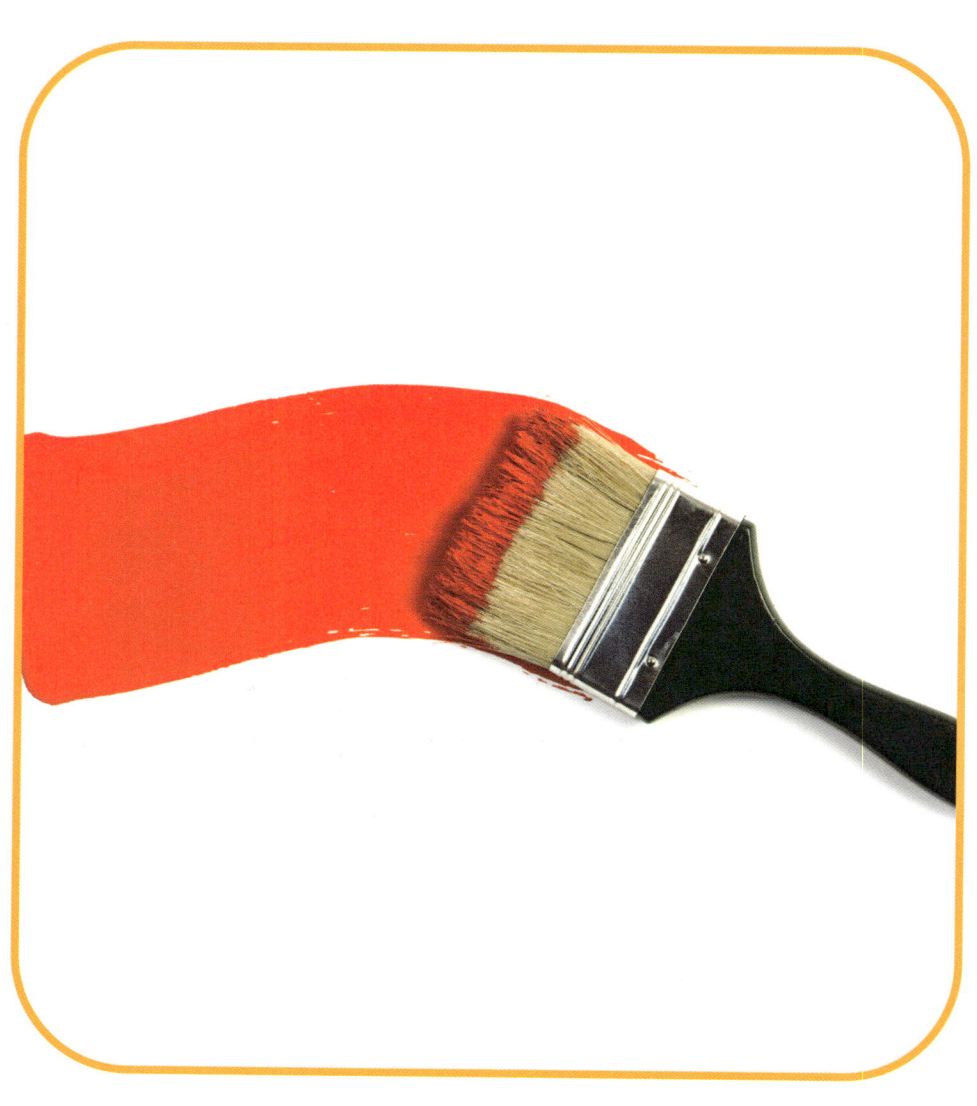

red

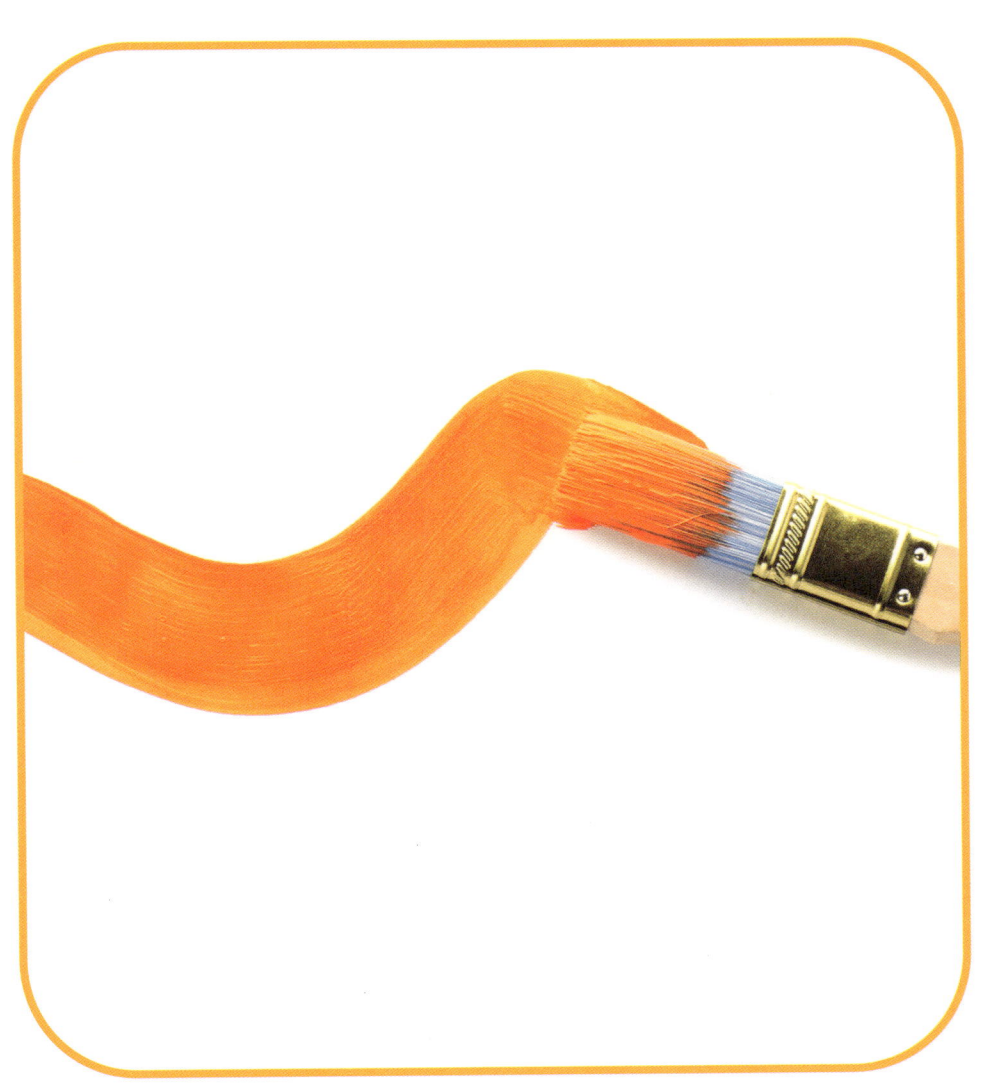

orange

yellow

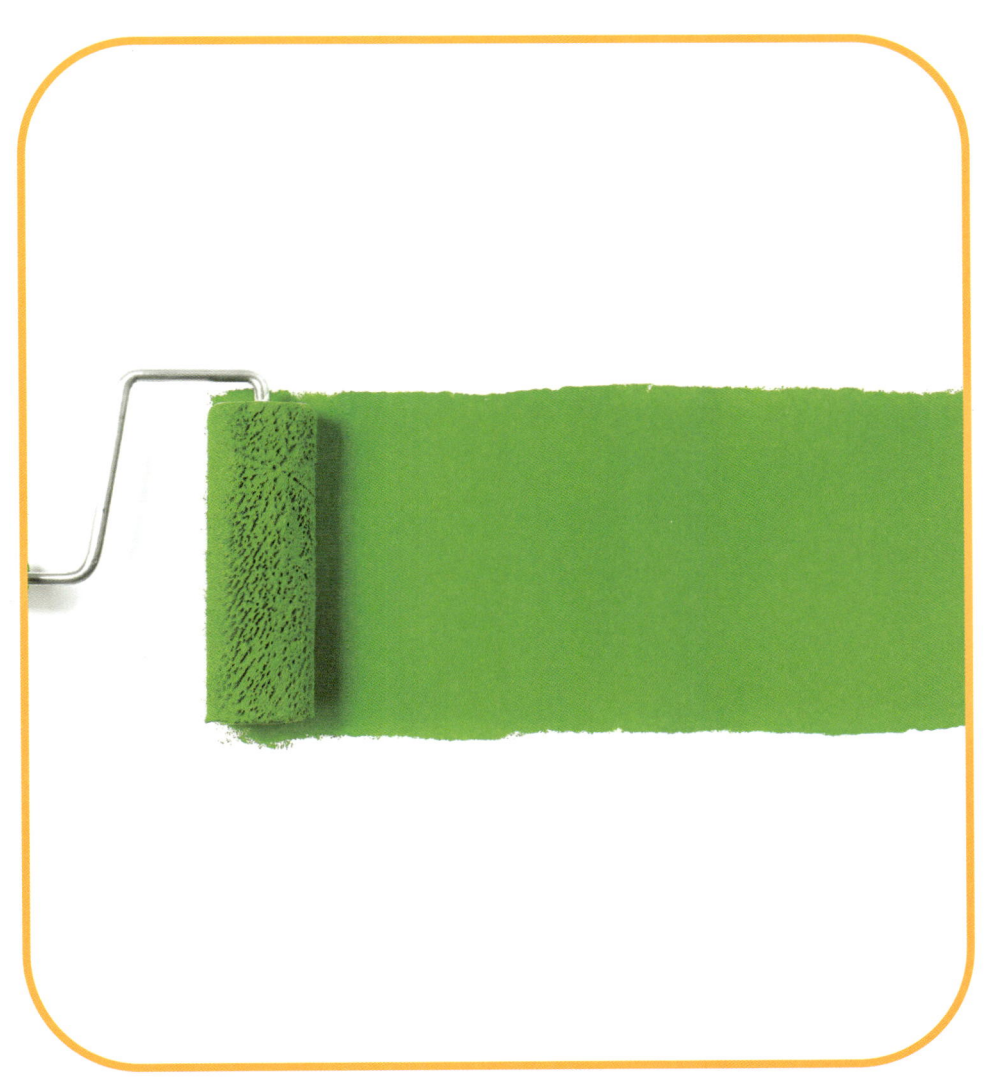

green

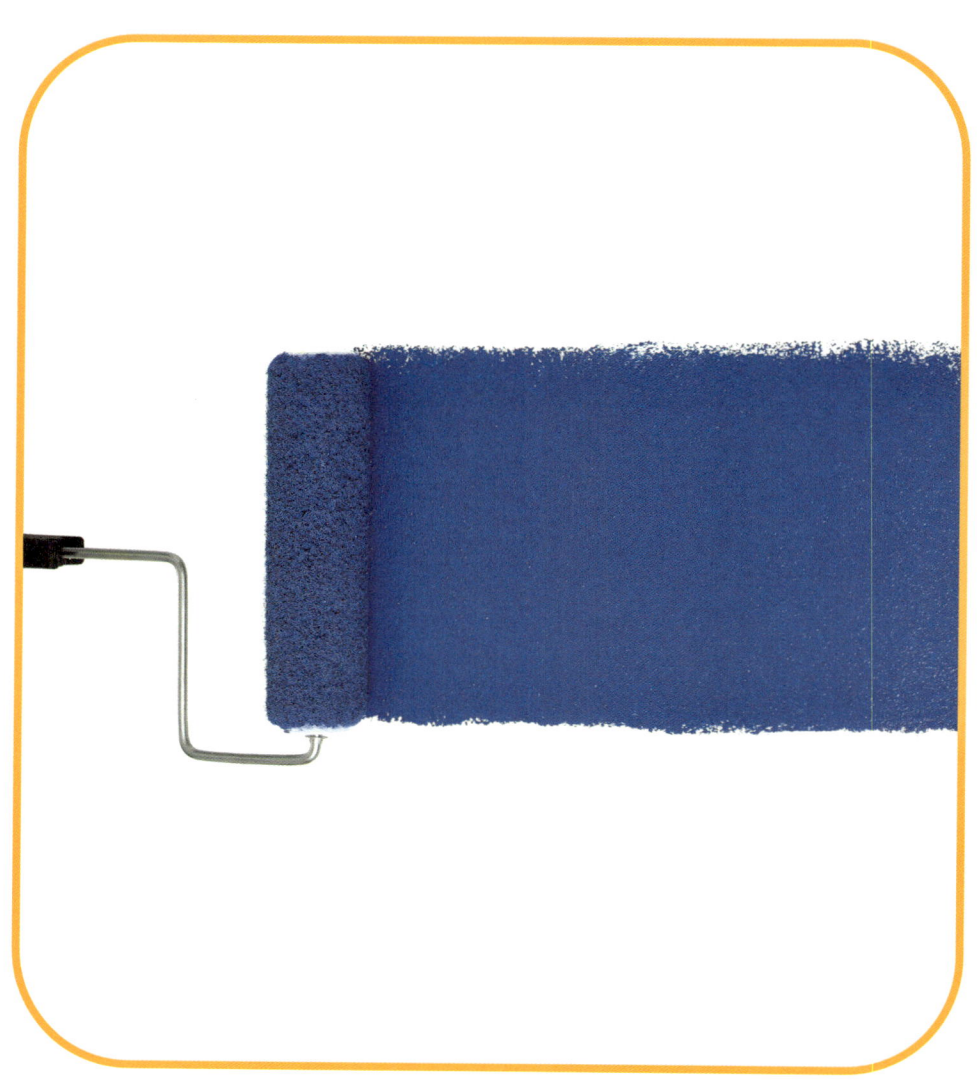

blue

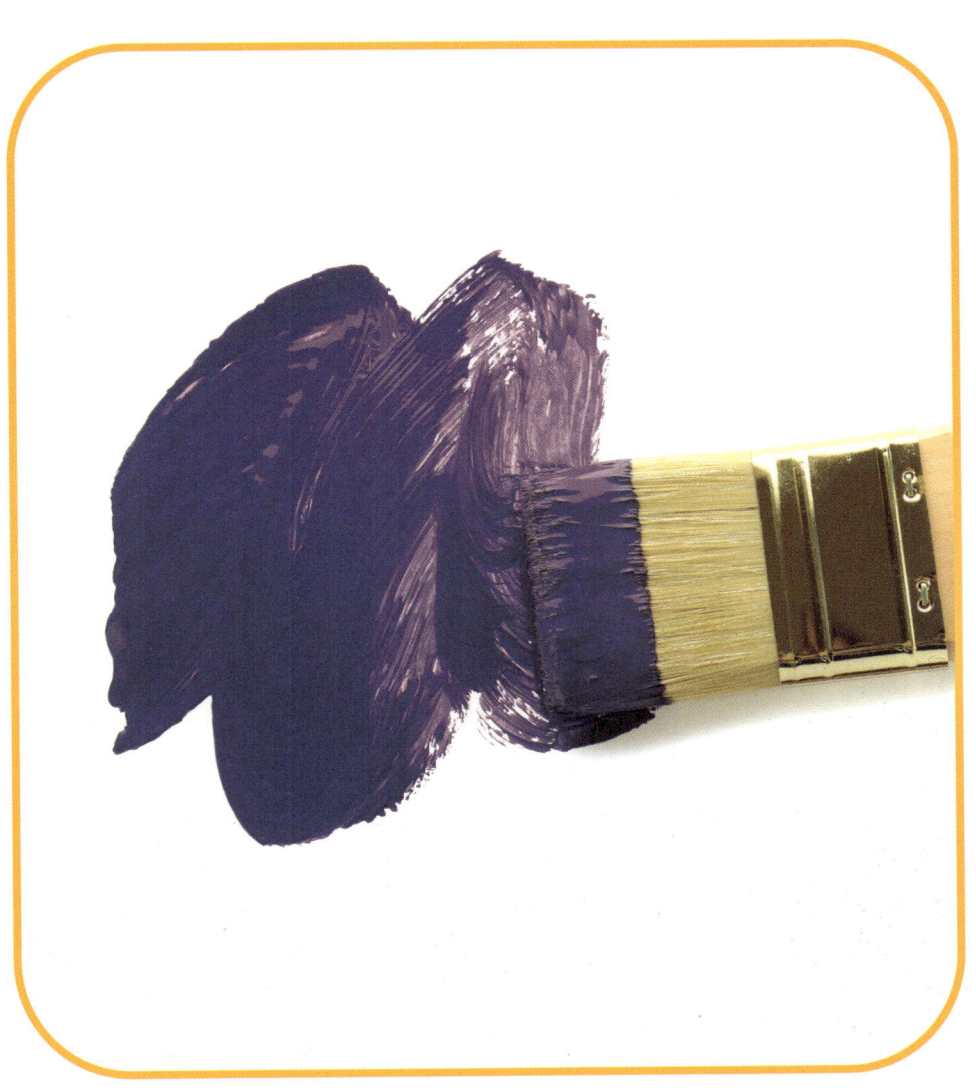

purple

black

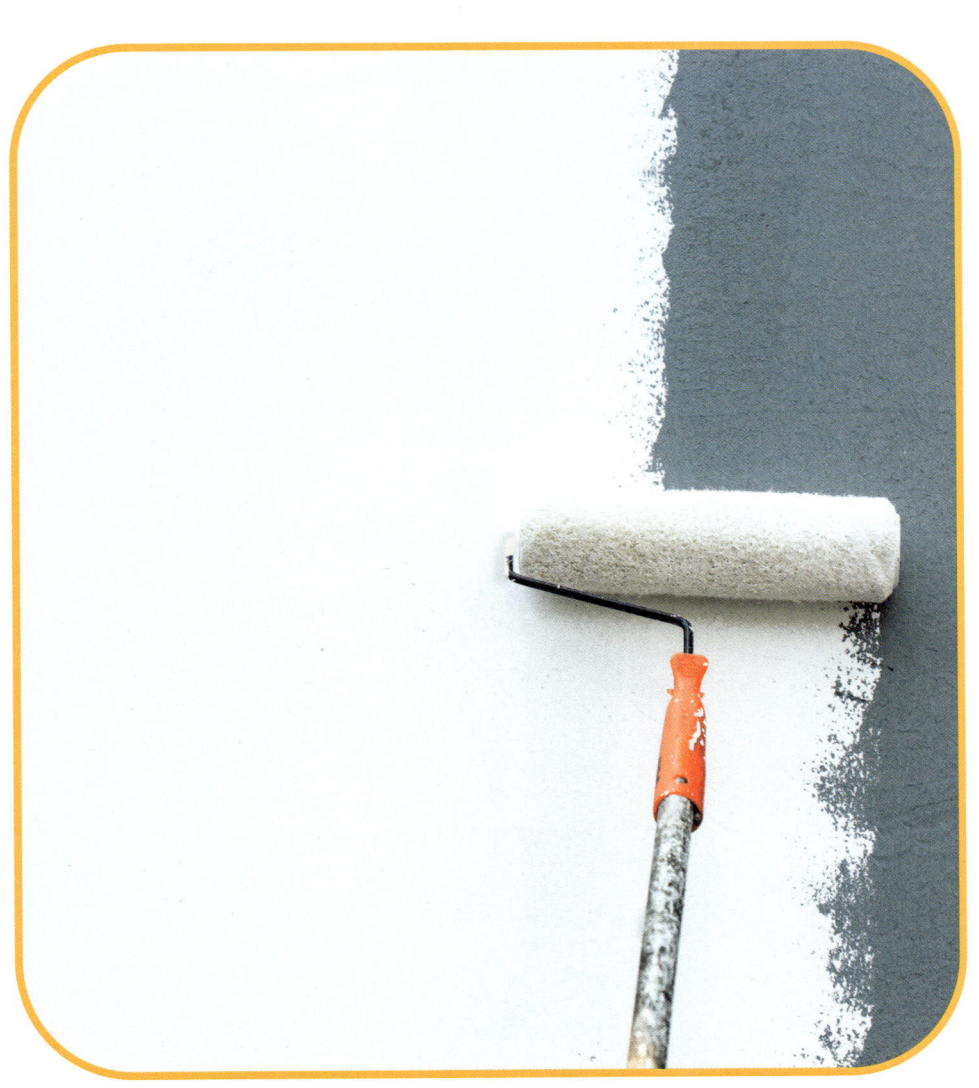

white

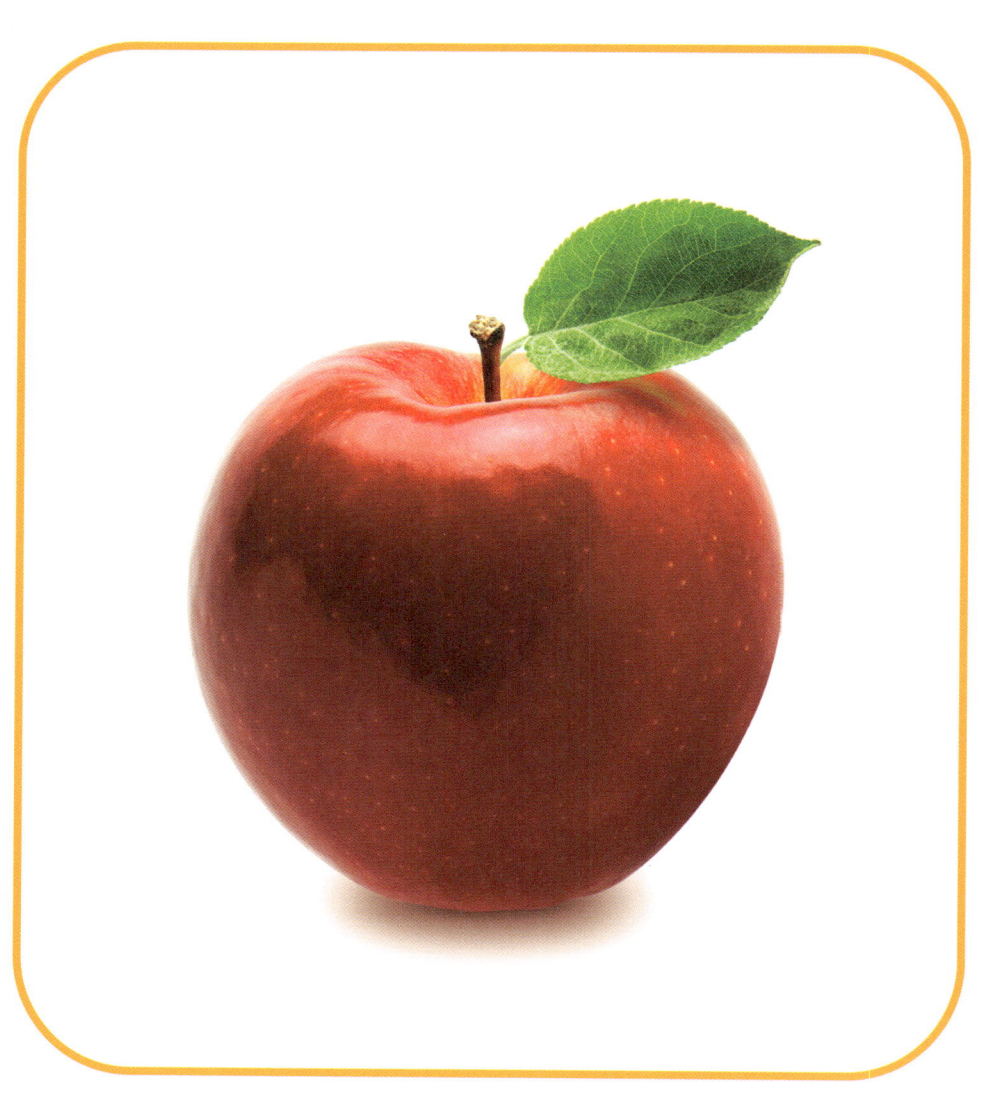

What color is it?

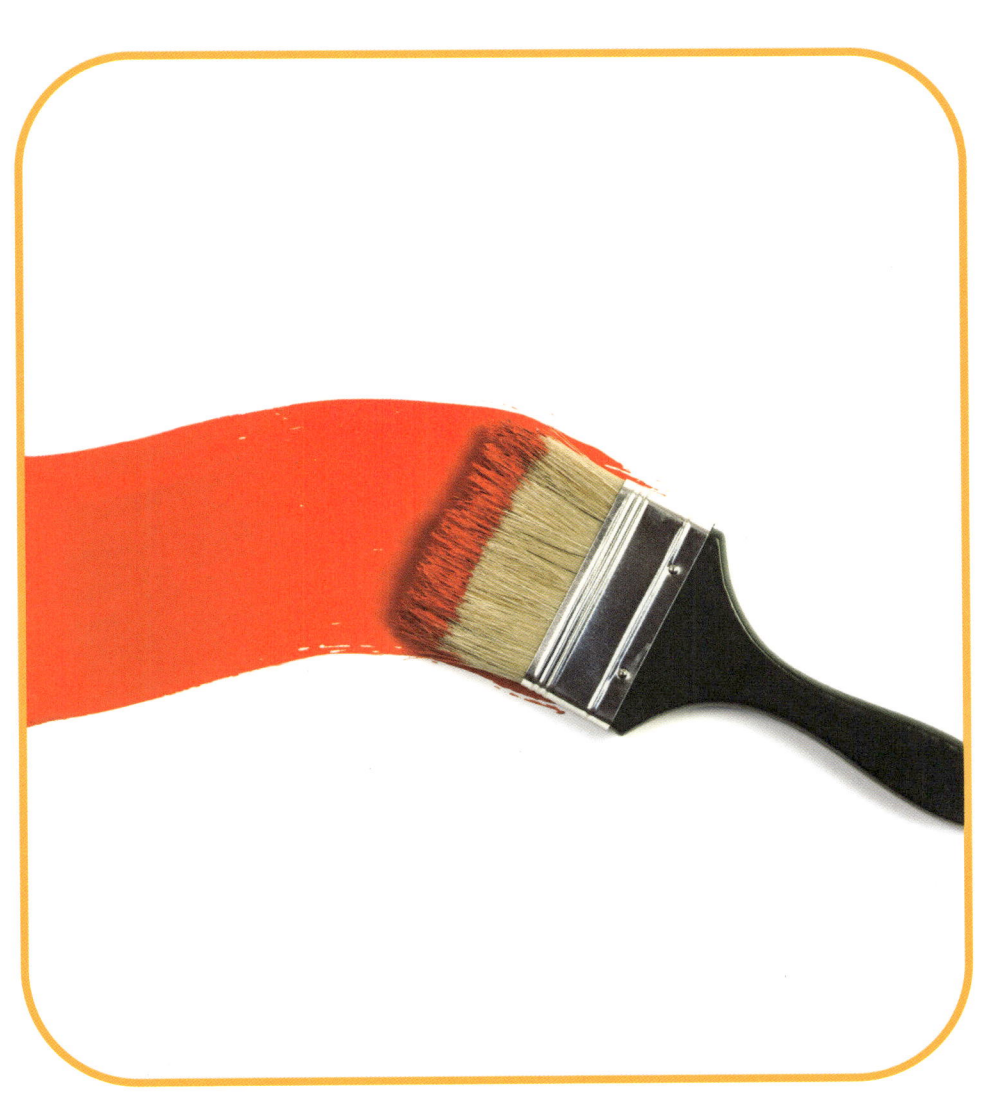

It's red.

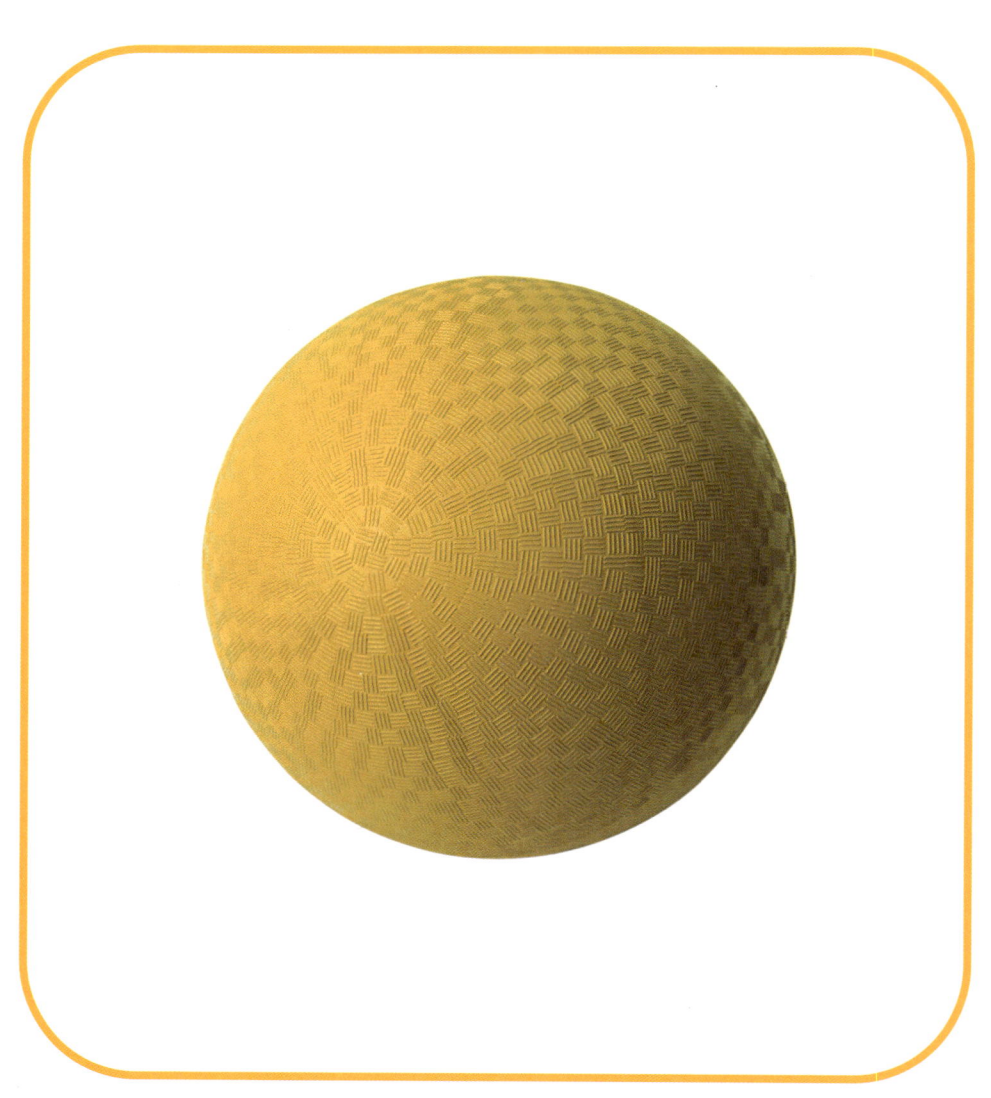

What color is it?

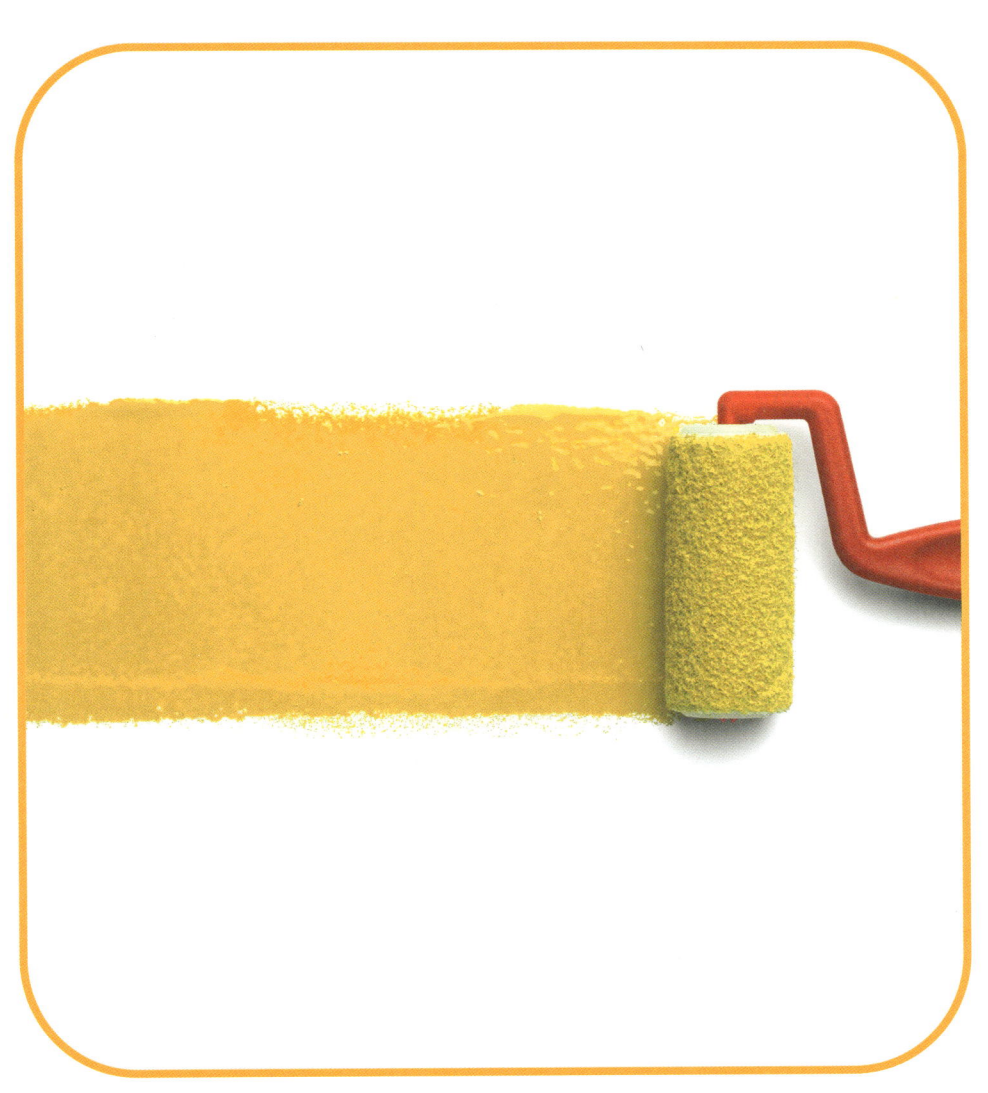

It's yellow.

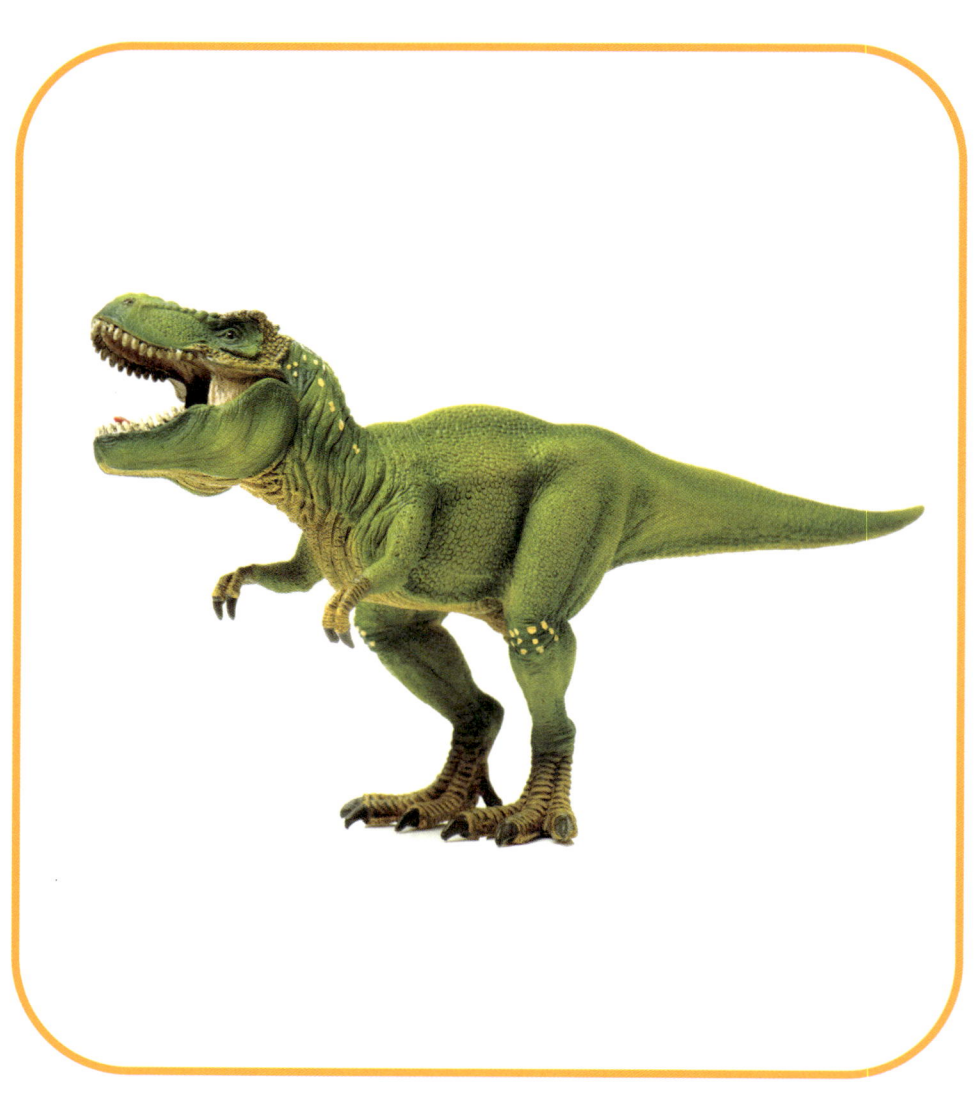

What color is it?

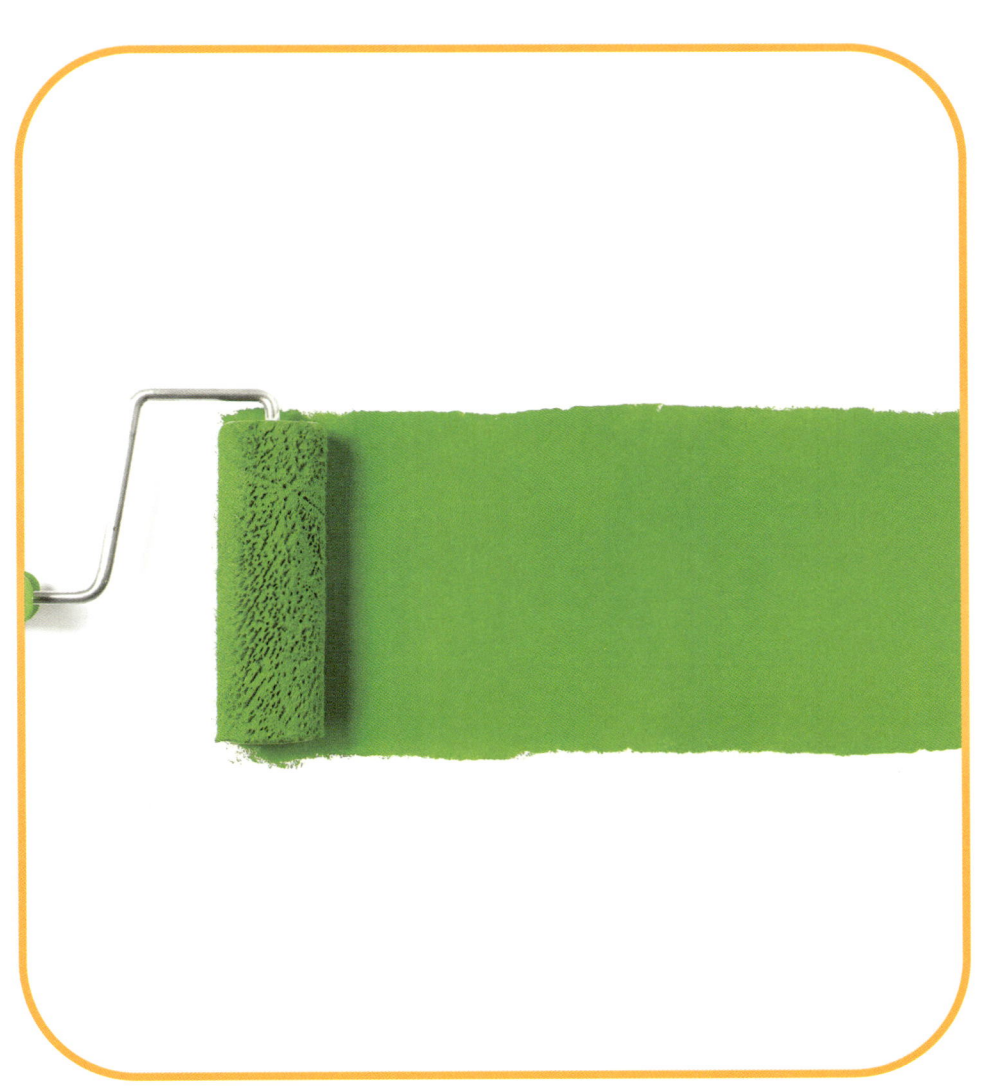

It's green.

Word List

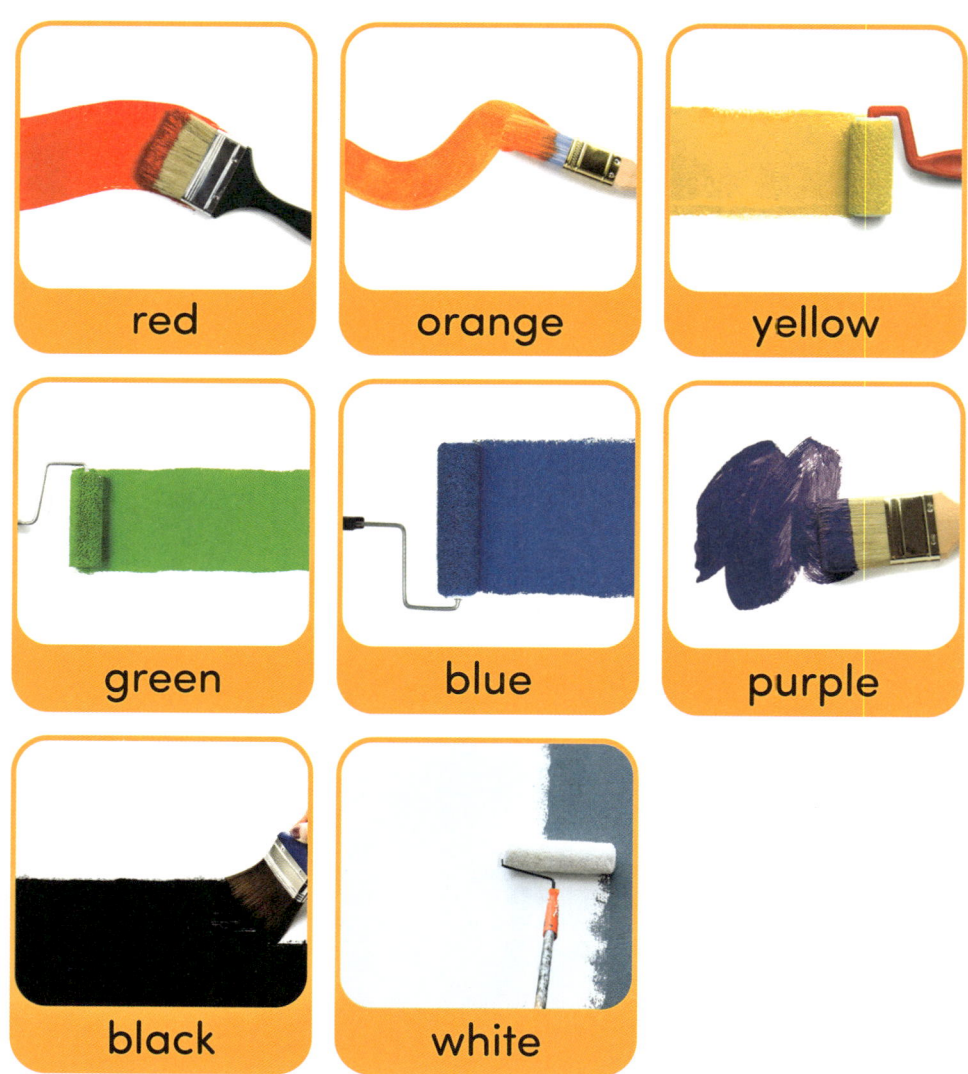

red

orange

yellow

green

blue

purple

black

white